MW01716683

The Expert's Guide to Writing a CV

How to highlight your skills, impress recruiters, and land your dream role

Emma Alkirwi

the CV guru

Cover and book design by Melvin Creative Ltd

Published by The CV Guru
Printed by Amazon.co.uk
Printed in Great Britain

ISBN 978-1-3999-7759-3

The Expert's Guide to Writing a CV

CONTENTS

Introduction 06

About The CV Guru 07

1 CV Fundamentals 09
> Tone 10
> CV Length 11
> Key Points to Keep in Mind 11
> Keywords and ATS 12

2 The Components of a CV 15
> CV Layout 16
> Experience 17
> Key Skills 20
> Education / Training / Certifications 21
> Additional Information 22
> Professional Profile 23
> Final Steps 24
> Tailoring Your CV 26
> Word Bank 28
> What Not to Include 29

3 Full CV Example 31

4 The Expert's Guide to Cover Letters 35

5 Key Terms 41

6 Appendix: Examples of Professional Profiles and Key Skills by Industry 42
> Account Management/Business Development / Sales 44
> Administration 45
> Construction/Labourer 46
> Driving 47
> First Job 48
> Graduate 49
> Hospitality 50
> Management 51
> Retail 52
> Warehouse/Production 53

INTRODUCTION

Thank you for purchasing this book!

This guide will teach you how to create an effective CV that impresses recruiters, wins job interviews, and helps you take your next step on the career ladder.

In this guide, I will go through the key sections on your CV and provide top tips on how to write each one in a way that grabs employers' attention and effectively highlights what you have to offer. Plus, I'll include real-life examples that you can use to improve your current CV.

I will also share current best practices with you, information on what not to include on your CV, and some advice on how to write a complementary Cover Letter to really make a great first impression.

With that in mind, let's get started!

Emma Alkirwi

Managing Director, The CV Guru

ABOUT THE CV GURU

Before founding The CV Guru, I spent fifteen years working in recruitment and the welfare-to-work industry.

During my time in these industries, I became frustrated as I watched many people fail to secure interviews for roles they would have excelled in. I realised that the problem always came back to the composition of their CV - the information that was included, how it was presented, and whether it was targeted to each specific role.

Oftentimes, people can struggle to talk about themselves and their experience in an objective manner. This means they are underselling themselves in their CV and falling at the first hurdle of the job application process.

In a competitive job market, you need to stand out. I founded The CV Guru in 2016, to provide job seekers with CVs, Cover Letters, and LinkedIn Profiles that are ATS-compliant and designed to stand out to their dream employer.

I am supported by a fantastic - and growing - team of experienced writers who support job seekers across a wide variety of industries.

We have a particular specialism in writing job application documents for those seeking out senior and executive-level positions, as well as those retiring from the police. We can also work directly with companies who sadly need to make employees redundant and provide professional documents to help them in their future job search.

You can find out more about us on our website: www.thecvguru.co.uk

Chapter One

CV Fundamentals

THE TONE OF YOUR CV

Striking the right tone in your CV is critical to making the best first impression.

Your CV should be written in the third person to sound professional. Avoid using words like "I" or "my", and don't refer to yourself by name either.

Here is an example to demonstrate this point.

Let's say you are applying for a role as a Customer Service Manager. In the Professional Profile section, instead of:

"I am a proactive Customer Service Manager and I have a proven track record of delivering an exceptional customer experience across luxury hospitality establishments."

You should write:

"A proactive Customer Service Manager with a proven track record of delivering an exceptional customer experience across luxury hospitality establishments."

And in the Career Summary section, instead of:

"I welcome guests to the restaurant and show them to their tables, then I explain the menu and learn about their dietary requirements."

It should be:

"Welcoming guests to the restaurant, showing them to their tables, explaining the menu, and making sure to understand their dietary requirements."

Your CV needs to be factual to the point, and professional. Avoid using casual language as much as possible. You can be more personal and include much more detail in your accompanying Cover Letter.

You should also ensure you don't use any filler words, such as:

> Really
> Very
> Exactly
> Just
> Almost
> Quite

These words don't add any meaning to the point you are trying to make, and can in fact dilute the impact of what you want to say.

THE LENGTH OF YOUR CV

In general, your CV should never be any more than two pages in length. There are a few exceptions to these guidelines:

School Leavers and Graduates: One-two pages, as you are likely to have less experience.

Contractors: Three pages, due to the variety of work you are likely to have undertaken.

WHAT TO KEEP IN MIND

Here are a few final points of consideration, before you start writing your CV:

1. **You need to tailor your CV for every position you apply for**. Sending a generic CV that doesn't pull out how your experience matches what the recruiter is looking for means you are putting yourself at a disadvantage at the very beginning of the application process.
2. **Keep the job advert handy.** Referring back to the job description repeatedly as you work through your CV is the easiest way to ensure you are writing in a way that meets the stated criteria.
3. **Ensure you understand ATS and Keywords.** Understanding keywords is critical to giving yourself the best chance of proceeding to the interview stage.

KEYWORDS AND APPLICANT TRACKING SOFTWARE

An important factor you need to consider when compiling your CV is Applicant Tracking Software, also known as ATS.

ATS is used predominantly by larger companies to shortlist suitable candidates for a position.

When your CV enters their software, the information within it is scanned to pre-populate their system.

Once a recruiter is ready to screen candidates' CVs, they will type in search words that are relevant to the position, and the CVs that include these terms will appear at the top of the results.

Those near the top of the search results are likely to have their documents read in full, which increases the chances of being invited to interview. If your CV appears at the bottom of the list, the recruiter may assume that your experience and skills are not relevant, as you have not included the specific criteria they are looking for.

This may sound complicated, but there are simple tricks you can use to increase your chances of appearing at the top of the list.

The first place you should look for potential keywords is within the Job Description. I recommend printing out a copy and then, armed with a pen or a highlighter, going through it section by section.

Which words or phrases do you think that a recruiter would search for within the ATS to find suitable candidates? You will usually find the majority of this information within the description of the role's responsibilities, and the essential and desirable criteria they are looking for.

You should avoid focusing on soft skills, or generic phrases such as 'outgoing' or 'hard-working' - recruiters will be far more specific in their criteria.

Once you understand the kinds of keywords that a recruiter may be looking for, you should include them in your CV where possible. Your Professional Profile and your Key Skills sections are particularly good places to include this information.

> "This is why the format of your CV is really important too. It may be tempting to use an aesthetically pleasing template that includes lots of imagery, but none of this content will be scannable - which means, if the company you are applying for uses ATS, you could be missing out on some great opportunities."

NOTES

Chapter Two

The Components of a CV

YOUR CV LAYOUT

Here are all of the sections you should include in your CV:

> **Contact Info**
> **Professional Profile**
> **Key Skills**
> **Experience (Employment History/Work Experience/Career Summary)**
> **Education**

You can also include an optional **Additional Information** section.

I will break down what each of these sections is and the information you need to include within them as you work through this guide.

You can also find a handy definition of each of these terms at the back of this guide.

So know you will know what we will cover ... where shall we start?

Surprisingly, it's not at the beginning!

EXPERIENCE

When creating your CV, the best place to start is with your experience.

First things first, you need to decide what you are going to call this section of your CV. There are a couple of different options, depending on the stage you are at in your career:

> **Work Experience** - ideal for students or recent graduates who have had work placements, voluntary positions, or held entry-level roles.
> **Employment History** - preferable for those who have a few years of employment under their belt, and have held a few differently paid jobs.
> **Career Summary** - most suitable for those who have had a similar career path over several years, and have previously held relatively senior roles.

Once you have selected the most appropriate option, start putting this section together. You need to include the following information:

PRACTICAL DETAILS

"If you have a long working history, you don't need to list every single position you have held."

Starting with your most recent position, work your way through your professional experience. Include the month and year that you started and finished with each company, and also include any voluntary work or unemployment gaps, if applicable.

If you have a long working history, you don't need to list every single position you have held. The last 10 years of your experience will suffice unless you need to include earlier experience to support a career change. The most important thing is that the recruiter or employer gets a fuller sense of the work you have been doing, and understands the value you could bring to their team.

KEY ACHIEVEMENTS

Once you have laid all this out you should start thinking about any key achievements that you wish to highlight for each role.

This helps you stand out from other candidates and can help lead what you discuss at interview should you reach the next stage of the process.

BUT WHAT CLASSIFIES AS A KEY ACHIEVEMENT?

Here are a few questions to consider when thinking about yours:

Did you win any awards or get recognised for your performance in any way?

Have you generated additional sales or saved costs?

Did you work on special projects or initiatives?

Did you improve any processes?

Were you promoted?

Did you increase sales?

Once you have your list, you should present them like these examples for a **Retail Sales position**:

> Due to exceptional performance and dedication, was promoted from Sales Assistant to Team Leader within six months.

> Delivered consistently excellent customer service and achieved all performance targets, which culminated in being recognised as Employee of the Month several times.

> Reviewed current stock processes, identified fast and slow-moving stock, and incorporated improvements into the ordering processes which has prevented idle stock and maximised sales.

> Undertook a review of current filing processes and standardised the systems to ensure a consistent approach across all departments, which resulted in increased efficiencies and supported strategic decision-making.

Note: If you are just starting in your career and feel you don't have key achievements to include, don't worry. These become more important a bit later in your working life when you begin to look for senior-level roles.

CORE RESPONSIBILITIES

Next, you should include the responsibilities you held within each role.

This is a description of your day-to-day tasks within the role or voluntary position. Try and start each sentence within each position using a different word - I have included a word bank later on in the guide to assist with this.

Here are some specific examples that would be used for a **Customer Service role**:

> **Provided** exceptional customer service as part of processing car rentals and bookings for customers, including preparing relevant documentation and processing payments.

> **Documented** all customer details required for the completion of rental agreements and contracts including personal details, insurance, and other relevant information.

> **Promptly** and **professionally** handled enquiries via email and telephone while ensuring all information and questions were responded to in line with company policies and procedures.

> **Checked** vehicles out to customers, including providing vehicle information regarding damages and ensuring vehicles were inspected when they were returned and compared to condition records.

KEY SKILLS

Your Key Skills section should be placed after your Contact Information and Professional Profile. This is where you highlight the specific competencies you have that make you the ideal candidate for a role.

This section is essential to any high-quality CV and is one of the key areas that will catch the eye of a recruiter or employer and encourage them to read your CV in full.

Your Key Skills section is also important for passing the requirements of ATS (Applicant Tracking Software).

> "This is where you highlight the specific competencies you have that make you the ideal candidate for a role."

To make the most of this section, it is essential to review the specific job advert for the position you are interested in and mirror the skills required.

Your Key Skills section should be a maximum of six to eight bullet points, and each point should only include a couple of words.

Here is an example of an effective Key Skills section on a CV for someone with **General Manager experience**:

People Management	Recruitment, Training and Coaching
Strategy Development	Rota Creation and Labour Optimisation
Client Management	Sales and Business Development
Complaint Handling	Employee Relations

PROFESSIONAL PROFILE

> "Use your key skills to support you in identifying the points you should cover within your Professional Profile."

Your Professional Profile is essentially a summary that sits at the top of your CV. It should introduce who you are and highlight the most relevant experience and skills you have in line with the position you are applying for.

Your Professional Profile should be between six and eight lines long, so you need to be very strategic about the information you include.

Even though this is the first section of your CV, it should be the last section you write.

The reason for this is that once you have completed all the other parts of your CV, you will have a clear view of the kind of information you should be highlighting and the tone you should strike when writing.

Use your key skills to support you in identifying the points you should cover within your Professional Profile.

Here is an example to show how these two sections can relate to one another, based on a CV for a **General Manager role**:

A highly experienced Manager with a successful background overseeing **people**, **resources** and budgets to drive sales, reduce costs, and enhance customer service. Demonstrable experience in **recruiting**, **coaching** and **leading high-performing teams** in fast-paced, customer-driven environments to meet and exceed targets. Possesses a strong aptitude for devising and delivering robust **sales strategies**, **streamlining processes** and optimising revenue streams. A strong communicator who can quickly build and maintain collaborative working relationships with **customers** and stakeholders to deliver on company objectives.

KEY SKILLS

People Management	Recruitment, Training and Coaching
Strategy Development	Resource Management
Customer Service Excellence	Sales and Business Development
Process Creation and Improvement	Budget Control

FINAL STEPS

Congratulations - you should now have a solid first draft of your CV!

Remember that you need to adapt your Professional Profile for each role you apply for, to ensure you meet the requirements of the Job Description each time.

Here is a final checklist you should work through before you send off your CV as part of a job application:

- Revisit the Job Description and ensure that your CV reflects the relevant skills and experience that recruiters will be looking for.
- Edit your CV to check for spelling and grammar mistakes. We are all prone to errors, and if you miss some a recruiter may question your attention to detail!
- Check that all of the contact information you have included is accurate and up to date.
- Ask someone you trust to review your CV. This will provide a second pair of eyes for an overall sense check and a more objective perspective than you have. A fresh viewpoint helps you understand if you have missed anything important that could help you stand out as a candidate.

HOW TO TAILOR YOUR CV FOR EACH ROLE

> "Use your key skills to support you in identifying the points you should cover within your Professional Profile."

The advice given throughout this guide will help you to write an interview-winning CV. However, one thing you need to keep in mind is that **you will need to make slight adaptions to it for every job you apply for**.

Tailoring your CV for each position helps you show how relevant your experience is, and how suitable you are for the role. If you send a generic CV that doesn't answer the specifications within the job description, you are unlikely to impress a prospective employer.

Don't worry: you don't need to rewrite the entire thing! The core of your CV will largely remain the same. The areas you will likely need to edit are your **Professional Profile** and **Key Skills** sections.

Here is how you should adapt each one:

PROFESSIONAL PROFILE

This is probably one of the most important areas to amend for the positions you are applying for - even if it's just a small tweak or two.

Study the job advert and ensure that the attributes required are highlighted in your Professional Profile. This will also help you to pass the Applicant Tracking Systems (ATS) check, as you will have included the specific keywords in the job description.

KEY SKILLS

This section is a good way for recruiters to see at a glance that you meet the role criteria, and also significantly supports you in getting past ATS. Study the skills required in the job advert and make sure these are mirrored in your Key Skills.

For example, you might be qualified for both a Customer Service position and a Sales role, but your Key Skills section needs to look different for each of these roles.

You can find a variety of examples of Key Skills and Professional Profiles, tailored to different roles, in the Appendix at the end of this guide.

If you are applying for a career change or a graduate/internship role, you may wish to format your CV a little differently.

The above still applies but within the Career Summary/Work Experience area, create a section for 'Relevant Work Experience' and bring your positions up front so the recruiter can immediately see the valuable experience you have that relates to the position you plan on transitioning to or applying for.

WORD BANK

Analysed	Conducted	Calculated
Compiled	Completed	Created
Devised	Delivered	Developed
Distributed	Documented	Evaluated
Enabled	Ensured	Formed
Gathered	Generated	Guided
Identified	Improved	Initiated
Introduced	Investigated	Led
Leveraged	Managed	Monitored
Negotiated	Organised	Oversaw
Planned	Presented	Promptly
Provided	Reviewed	Revised
Selected	Spearheaded	Streamlined
Supported	Surpassed	Taught
Trained	Transformed	Wrote

WHAT NOT TO INCLUDE ON YOUR CV

So far, we have covered all of the information you should include on your CV.

However, there are also several pieces of information you should not include:

A Photograph

In the UK, you are not required to have a photograph on your CV, unless you are applying for acting or modelling roles. Including one can be distracting - how you look is not relevant to your ability to do a job.

As mentioned previously, images also aren't scannable by ATS, so including a photograph could hinder your chances of reaching the next stages of application.

An Unprofessional Email Address

If you're still using a childhood email address or one that includes the name of your favourite football team, you need to create a new one before you start your job hunt!

Ensure the email address you include is simple, to avoid potential spelling mistakes on the recruiter's side. I advise where possible to just include your first and last name in your email address.

Your Date of Birth

This is no longer a requirement on your CV, so I recommend you do not include it. The reason for this is to avoid age discrimination of any kind, be it accidental or deliberate. Simply focus on your skills and experience instead.

Your Marital Status

Your marital status does not have an impact on your ability to do a job well, and so there is no place for it on your CV.

Your Education Dates

Similar to your DOB, including your education dates could lead to age discrimination. Unless you are a current student or a new graduate, simply state what you studied, where you did it, and the qualification you obtained.

Your References

This might surprise you, but it's true!

It is advisable to include the phrase *"References are available upon request"* at the end of your CV, but you should not feature full names, addresses, and phone numbers as part of your initial application.

Including personal information like this could lead to referees being contacted unnecessarily, which could irritate them and may result in an unfavourable reference.

Chapter Three
Full CV Example

Robert
Smith

07707 555 888
London, UK
robert.smith@smith.com
robert-smith

Professional Profile

A customer focused and commercially astute individual with a proven track record working as a Manager within reputable and luxury hotels. Obtained comprehensive operational experience and has successfully devised strategies to increase profit, reduce costs and increase overall customer satisfaction. Possesses sound financial awareness and can confidently review forecasts, profit and loss accounts and managing labour costs against sales. Demonstrable experience promoting high standards with staff with the ability to train and develop people across all aspects of hospitality functions. Displays strong communication skills both verbal and written and is up to date with social media and review platforms to manage the hotels brand and reputation.

Key Skills

People Management and Development
Labour Management Optimisation
Health and Safety
Customer Service Excellence
Driving Financial Performance
Coaching, Training and People Development
Continuous Improvement Approach
Food and Beverage Management

Career Summary

CHELTENHAM LUXURY HOTEL **2016 – present**
General Manager **2017 – present**
Key Achievements:

- Due to exceptional performance in previous role was appointed the General Manager of the hotel and have continually engaged with the local business community to increase the hotel's visibility and popularity.
- Restructured the restaurant and bar departments which resulted in savings of £100k per annum and during Christmas 2021 exceeded revenue targets across Meetings and Events by over £40k.
- Successfully led the team in March 2023 during Race Week and achieved an £8k increase in room sales than the previous year including record sales on the final day of the races.
- Managed the process of the refurbishment of 61 bedrooms while the hotel remained open, coordinated the contract transition with the central HR team from the previous hotel company, and aligned employee benefits across hotel staff.

Responsibilities:

- Partnering with local charities to increase the hotels social media exposure to drive local footfall into the hotel and continually working with conference and events to assist them in targeting local companies.
- Analysing and monitoring the financial performance of the hotel including reviewing profit across key events, weekly and seasonal trends as well as performance by rooms, restaurant, bar and meetings and events.
- Providing regular reports to area management regarding the performance and profitability of the hotel and ensuring all departments exceed their targets.
- Managing all recruitment and training requirements for the hotel including interviewing, training and developing staff to high standards to ensure exceptional customer service.
- Actively seeking feedback from guests to foster a continuous improvement approach and efficiently handling any guest complaints verbally and in writing to maintain and protect the reputation of the hotel.
- Ensuring all staff complete necessary training in line with standards and obligations to support a positive health and safety culture to target a zero-incident record, ensuring the establishment complies with all licensing laws.

Deputy General Manager **2016 – 2017**
Key Achievements:

- Successfully adapted to the hotel brand through pro-actively learning about the local area and grasping the culture of the brand and its' positioning within the local area.
- Implemented crisis management procedures and ensured that all key management and supervisors were trained and fully understood their responsibilities and obligations.

Page 1

Career Summary *(continued.)*

- Enhanced the hotel's Twitter profile by increasing followers through partnering with key influencers within Cheltenham to increase the hotel's image and footfall.
- Significantly contributed to the re-branding of the hotel by ensuring the hotel culture and standards are visual throughout the hotel including instilling key aspects into staff conduct, attitude and performance.

Responsibilities:

- Responsible for overseeing all activities to contribute to the successful running of the hotel covering 61 bedrooms, three functions rooms, the restaurant and bar to ensure revenues are maximised at all opportunities.
- Working alongside the Sales Manager, Financial Controller, and General Manager to prepare the room occupancy forecast, and revenue management to ensure profits are maximised.
- Acting as General Manager when required, recruiting and training staff, conducting performance reviews, handling with any disciplinary and grievance matters and ensuring the hotel's brand standards are practiced by all staff.

FOUR STAR HOTEL — **2013 – 2016**
Deputy General Manager
Key Achievements:

- Approached by the regional operational manager to work in another hotel site due to operational problems within the hotel and due to the success was offered the role.
- Responsible for increasing the e-learning score of the hotel from 37% to 92% and assisted in moving Review Pro Percentage up to 95% which are both ranking second within the brand.
- Health and safety advocate for the company and increased score from 68% to 92% and currently achieving above the brand average of 85% consistently for the past 6 months.
- Created a positive up-selling culture within the hotel to enhance the guests' experience and increase the financial performance of the hotel.
- Selected to go to Winchester as a trouble shooter to assist in staff training, promote up-selling and share best practice.

SCOTTISH FOUR STAR HOTEL — **2012 – 2013**
Restaurant and Bar Manager
Key Achievements:

- Increasing the rating on Trip Advisor of the Brasserie and Bar from number 88 to 52 out of 265 restaurants and bars in Dundee within a three month period.
- Retaining a gross profit of 72% every month by reducing holding stock and upselling packages at weddings and other events.

FOUR STAR COUNTRY HOTEL — **2003 – 2012**
Assistant Food and Beverage Manager — **2010 – 2012**
Guest Services Manager — **2008 – 2010**
Restaurant Supervisor — **2003 – 2008**

Education, Qualifications and Training

Certifications: SVQ Level 4 in Management (2013), Food and Hygiene Certificate-Level 3 (2013), First Aid Trained, Personal License Holder, Group Trainer Certified

References are available upon request

NOTES

Chapter Four

The Expert's Guide to Cover Letters

COVER LETTERS

> "A Cover Letter will also enable a recruiter or employer to understand your transferable skills and why you are suitable for the role."

In the majority of cases, you will expected to send a Cover Letter alongside your CV to apply for a position. Although this guide focuses on how to write a CV, I thought it was important to give you some tips on how to create an effective Cover Letter that complements the detail you have included within it.

Taking the time to compile a Cover Letter demonstrates your commitment and interest in the role, and also allows you to expand on points you could not cover fully on your CV in more detail.

A Cover Letter will also enable a recruiter or employer to understand your transferable skills and why you are suitable for the role.

Before you start make sure to thoroughly review the Job Description, research the company to understand their values, and examine the Person Specification within the job listing. Write some notes on how you align, and have this on hand when writing your Cover Letter to ensure you don't miss any important points.

When writing your Cover Letter make sure to:

> Continuously refer to your CV, to keep the tone and language aligned across both documents.

> Follow any guidance provided by the company, such as character limits.

> Check the font size and colour match your CV.

> Make sure you triple-check for any spelling or grammar errors.

> Avoid abbreviations.

Here is an example to show you how you should structure your Cover Letter.

How to structure a cover letter

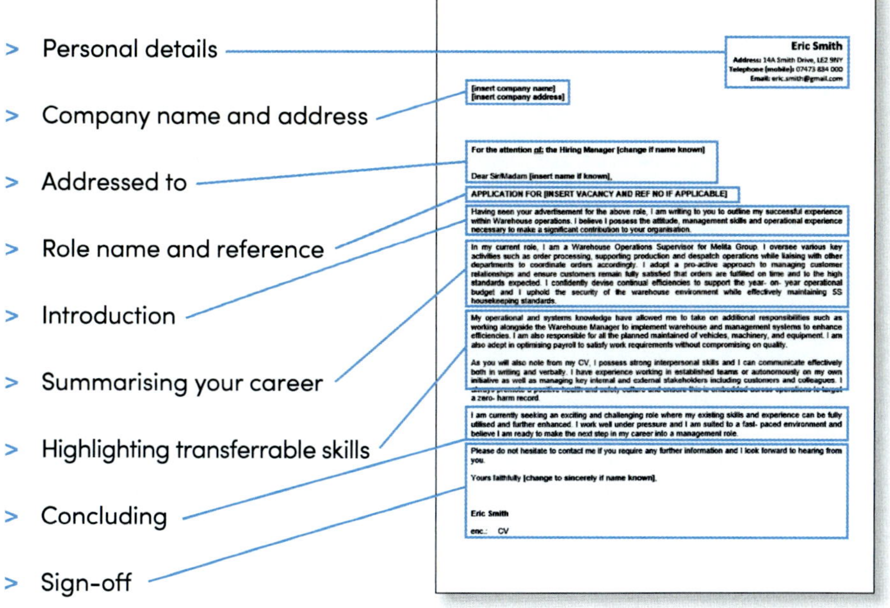

Eric Smith
Address: 14A Smith Drive, LE2 9NY
Telephone (mobile): 07473 834 000
Email: eric.smith@gmail.com

[insert company name]
[insert company address]

For the attention of: the Hiring Manager [change if name known]

Dear Sir/Madam [insert name if known],

APPLICATION FOR [INSERT VACANCY AND REF NO IF APPLICABLE]

Having seen your advertisement for the above role, I am writing to you to outline my successful experience within Warehouse operations. I believe I possess the attitude, management skills and operational experience necessary to make a significant contribution to your organisation.

In my current role, I am a Warehouse Operations Supervisor for Melita Group. I oversee various key activities such as order processing, supporting production and despatch operations while liaising with other departments to coordinate orders accordingly. I adopt a pro-active approach to managing customer relationships and ensure customers remain fully satisfied that orders are fulfilled on time and to the high standards expected. I confidently devise continual efficiencies to support the year- on- year operational budget and I uphold the security of the warehouse environment while effectively maintaining 5S housekeeping standards.

My operational and systems knowledge have allowed me to take on additional responsibilities such as working alongside the Warehouse Manager to implement warehouse and management systems to enhance efficiencies. I am also responsible for all the planned maintained of vehicles, machinery, and equipment. I am also adept in optimising payroll to satisfy work requirements without compromising on quality.

As you will also note from my CV, I possess strong interpersonal skills and I can communicate effectively both in writing and verbally. I have experience working in established teams or autonomously on my own initiative as well as managing key internal and external stakeholders including customers and colleagues. I a zero- harm record.

I am currently seeking an exciting and challenging role where my existing skills and experience can be fully utilised and further enhanced. I work well under pressure and I am suited to a fast- paced environment and believe I am ready to make the next step in my career into a management role.

Please do not hesitate to contact me if you require any further information and I look forward to hearing from you.

Yours faithfully [change to sincerely if name known].

Eric Smith

enc.: CV

I recommend mirroring the example above when creating the first draft of your Cover Letter, as it includes all of the sections that the reader will be expecting to see.

The first five sections - **'Personal details', company name and address'**, **'addressed to'**, **'role name and reference'**, and **'introduction'**, are all fairly straightforward to complete.

Once these are done, you need to move on to the **Career Summary** section.

Here is the key information you need to include in this section:

> The skills and experience they have asked for in the Job Advert, with relevant examples where possible;

> Descriptions of your skills and experience using the keywords that are included in the Job Advert.

Next, you should write a paragraph that highlights your transferable skills.

Here are some top tips to help you do this:

- Refer back to the list of your key skills in line with the Job Description.
- Create sentences that will cover these noting the specifics of how these skills are transferable.
- Explain **why** these skills are transferrable with examples.
- Add in some more interpersonal skills and remember to include some of the softer skills from the job description too.

Check out the example below, which illustrates how to do this effectively:

My operational and systems knowledge have allowed me to take on additional responsibilities such as working alongside the Warehouse Manager to implement warehouse and management systems to enhance efficiencies. I am also responsible for all planned maintenance of vehicles, machinery, and equipment. I am also adept in optimising payroll to satisfy work requirements without compromising on quality.

As you will note from my CV, I possess strong interpersonal skills and I can communicate effectively both in writing and verbally. I have experience working in established teams or autonomously on my own initiative as well as managing key internal and external stakeholders including customers and colleagues. I always promote a positive health and safety culture and ensure this is embedded across operations to target a zero-harm record.

Finally, you need to sign off and close your Cover Letter in a professional and engaging way.

A great way to do this that provides another example of your interest in the role is to do some additional research and say something that is specifically tailored to the company.

You could use language such as:

"Having undertaken some research into the company..."

"I have reviewed your company website and see you have won an award for customer service..."

You should also include a standard closing statement that says you are happy to send over any further information if it is required.

Then, you should sign off the letter professionally. If you do not know the name of the person you are writing to, you should use the phrase **"Yours faithfully"**. If you do know the name of the person you are writing to, change this to **"Yours sincerely"**.

Here is a final example to illustrate how to structure this section:

I am currently seeking an exciting and challenging role where my existing skills and experience can be fully utilised and further enhanced. I work well under pressure and I am suited to a fast-paced environment and believe I am ready yo make the next step in my career into a management role.

Please do not hesitate to contact me if you require any further information and I look forward to hearing from you.

Yours faithfully [change to sincerely if name known}.

NOTES

Chapter Five
Key Terms

ATS

Applicant Tracking Software, used by larger companies to shortlist suitable candidates for a position using key terms that have been included within the Job Description.

Education

The section which sits just below 'Experience' within your CV, and details your qualifications and the institutions you received them from.

Career Summary

The title of the 'Experience' section within the CV for those who have had a similar career path over several years and held relatively senior roles.

Cover Letter

An extended document that accompanies a CV as part of a job application, where you can expand on your relevant skills and experience.

CV

A document you prepare when applying for jobs which allows you to summarise your education, skills, and professional experience.

Employment History

The title of the 'Experience' section within the CV for those who have a few years of employment under their belt, and have held a few differently paid jobs.

Key Skills

A short section of between 6 and 8 bullet points, where you highlight the specific competencies you have that make you the ideal candidate for a role, in line with the job description.

Professional Profile

A summary that sits at the top of your CV of between six and eight lines long. It should introduce who you are and highlight your most relevant skills and experience.

Work Experience

The title of the 'Experience' section within the CV for students or recent graduates who have had work placements, voluntary positions, or held entry-level roles.

Chapter Six

Appendix:

Examples of Professional Profiles and Key Skills by Industry

ACCOUNT MANAGEMENT/ BUSINESS DEVELOPMENT/SALES

PROFESSIONAL PROFILE

An accomplished Business Development professional with a proven track record driving sales growth, providing technical solutions to clients, and managing the full sales lifecycle. Possesses demonstrable experience adapting sales technique to secure new clients while up/cross selling solutions. Adopts a pro-active approach to understanding clients' challenges to inform product options and technical solutions. Utilises market knowledge to ensure solutions are complete and deliver on client objectives. Works effectively to build long lasting relationships through acting as a trusted associate.

KEY SKILLS

Sales and Business Development

Relationship Management

Pipeline Management

Coaching and Mentoring

Account Management

Pipeline Management

Pricing and Negotiation

CRM Knowledge and Expertise

NOTES

ADMINISTRATION

PROFESSIONAL PROFILE

A meticulous and efficient professional with comprehensive experience gained in customer service and administration. Possesses excellent organisational and communication skills with the ability to complete tasks in constrained timescales. Learns work procedures and practices quickly including company specific processes. Displays an excellent telephone manner and is confident in completing invoicing, database management and correspondence. Able to build rapport leading to lasting collaborative relationships. Fits well into already established teams and enjoys taking on additional responsibilities.

KEY SKILLS

Customer Service Management

Excellent Telephone Manner

Confidential Administration

Continuous Improvement Approach

Invoicing and Reports

Database Management

Correspondence

First Aid

NOTES

CONSTRUCTION/LABOURER

PROFESSIONAL PROFILE

An experienced Labourer who has gained substantial experience within various companies. Operated successfully across construction sites including handling small tools, plant and machinery. Completes work to an extremely high standard while working to strict specifications. Committed to health and safety including adhering to strict site safety standards, method statements, and risk assessments. Works well across trades and collaborates well with suppliers and contractors in line with agreed work scope, quality standards and engineering drawings.

KEY SKILLS

Health and Safety	Labouring
Glazier	Site and Material Preparation
Installation of Glazed Units	Groundwork

NOTES

DRIVING

PROFESSIONAL PROFILE

A customer service focused professional who has gained substantial experience working within driving and customer service focused positions. Possesses a proven track record of working to set company processes and procedures while ensuring compliance to health and safety regulations. Confidently plans routes ensuring timescales are achieved. Learns company processes and procedures quickly and with ease and fits well into teams. Displays strong communication skills both verbal and in writing and works collaboratively with internal departments.

KEY SKILLS

Good Geographical Knowledge

....

Vehicle Maintenance

....

Route Optimisation

....

Health and Safety

....

Solution Focused

....

Positive Company Advocate

....

NOTES

FIRST JOB

PROFESSIONAL PROFILE

An eager individual who is currently seeking first opportunity into the workplace. Enjoys being part of a team and can work well on own initiative. A quick learner and is keen to understand the everyday working practices of the **customer service industry***. Strives to achieve the highest standards and understands the importance of health and safety within the workplace. Happy to undertake further training in order to develop my experience.

*You can change customer service industry to what you are seeking.

KEY SKILLS

IT Literate	Quick Learner
Strong Communication Skills	Customer Service Knowledge
Key Team Player	Problem Solving Skills

NOTES

GRADUATE

PROFESSIONAL PROFILE

A logical and methodical Undergraduate with an exceptional academic record and a range of practical work experience. Effectively balances a wide range of tasks and delivers against multiple deadlines. Passionate about developing an understanding into the structure, culture and procedures of project management. Successfully builds professional relationships and displays confident communication skills. Learns new work procedures and practices quickly while always acting as a positive advocate of the organisation. Currently seeking project management work experience that offers an opportunity to obtain practical skills.

KEY SKILLS

Customer Service Excellence

Relationship Management

Report Writing

Task and Project Management

Continuous Improvement

Presentations

NOTES

HOSPITALITY

PROFESSIONAL PROFILE

A customer focused hospitality professional with valuable experience working within various restaurants. Serves food and beverages to a high standard while understanding customer specifications or allergens. Delivers an exceptional customer service experience and utilises opportunities to up-sell without compromising the service. Actively promotes high food quality and service standards in line with best practice. Entrusted to train and develop staff to ensure brand standards are achieved. Builds long term relationships with customers, colleagues and suppliers.

KEY SKILLS

Health and Hygiene	Customer Service Excellence
Cash Handling	Reception Duties
Personal Licence Holder	Supporting Events

NOTES

MANAGEMENT

PROFESSIONAL PROFILE

An accomplished and dynamic Manager with a track record leading teams, driving KPI and financial performance, and delivering the organisational strategy. Successfully increased sales, reduced costs, and improved processes through building a high performing team and enhancing customer service standards. Demonstrable experience motivating teams including encouraging a coaching and learning environment in line with company culture. An effective communicator who works collaboratively with colleagues and suppliers, and key stakeholders.

KEY SKILLS

People Management	Recruitment, Training and Coaching
Strategy Development	Rota Creation and Labour Optimisation
Client Management	Sales and Business Development
Complaint Handling	Employee Relations

NOTES

RETAIL

PROFESSIONAL PROFILE

A customer service focused individual who has substantial experience working within the fashion industry. Committed to achieving and exceeding targets while remaining focused on providing an exceptional standard of service to a wide range of customers. Highly organised, possesses a logical and methodical approach to any task undertaken and completes all tasks quickly and efficiently. Successfully managed retail operations, inventory, and merchandising in line with brand standards. Promotes customer service excellence while creating a positive environment to increase sales and achieve ambitious retail targets.

KEY SKILLS

Visual Merchandising	Customer Service
Cash Handling	Coaching and Mentoring Staff
Key Holder Duties	Target Focused

NOTES

WAREHOUSE/PRODUCTION

PROFESSIONAL PROFILE

A dedicated professional with valuable practical skills and experience in repair, maintenance, delivery driving and production. Able to work across warehousing/production environments in line with company processes and procedures. Adopts a pro-active approach to health and safety ensuring compliance with best practice. Committed to improving processes, reducing costs, and utilising technical skills to enhance quality standards through lean six sigma. Maintains internal documentation, systems, and processes as well as training and supporting colleagues.

KEY SKILLS

Customer Service Excellence	Health and Safety
Quality Control	Compliance
Record Keeping	Target Driven

NOTES

NOTES

Made in the USA
Las Vegas, NV
07 May 2026

46457526R00033